Search Engine Optimisation:

Best practice strategies to successfully promote your website online

Phil Robinson • Lindsey Annison
Foreword by Dave Chaffey

ClickThrough Marketing

ClickThrough
the search conversion experts

Search Engine Optimisation: Best practice strategies to successfully promote your website online, 1st Edition

Published by
ClickThrough Marketing,
Charter House, Sandford Street, Lichfield, WS13 6QA
www.clickthrough-marketing.com

First Published 2010

ISBN: 978-1-907603-00-6

For information on all ClickThrough Marketing publications and services please visit our website at http://www.clickthrough-marketing.com

ClickThrough Marketing can offer discounts on this book when ordered as a bulk purchase. For more information contact ClickThrough Marketing on 0800 088 7486 or email experts@clickthrough-marketing.com.

All images contained within this work are © iStockphoto.com.
Edited by John Newton.

ClickThrough
the search conversion experts

In my experience, success with SEO has 3 essential ingredients.

First, process. As with other digital marketing activities there are a lot of options available to improve SEO, so you need to carefully define what you're looking to achieve for your business and then line up the right tools to hit your targets.

Second, measurement. Meeting your goals means quality traffic, not just volume, so integrating the many fantastic analytics and insights sources that are available to marketers today and then reviewing and acting on the information regularly is also key to success.

Third, creativity. Success in SEO today requires outstanding content that will entertain, inform and be shared. So, creating a buzz through creating the right content for your audience and then connecting to influencers to share the story is what we strive for at ClickThrough Marketing.

We wanted our SEO 101 Guide to be different from the many dry, technical guides to SEO which you may have read in the past, instead highlighting the creative opportunities available. We also hope you'll find it to be a practical guide that you can use to check our tips against your current practice.

The guide will take you through a journey of what matters in search, starting with a review of the type of goals you should set and an introduction to the way search engines work to find your content and then rank it when searchers search.

We also show how you should go beyond plain text content to use rich media like images, social comments, maps and video to get in front of your prospects as they search through Google and the other search engines.

Throughout the guide you will find the focus is on the customer, with suggestions to find out how customers think, how they behave when they search and most importantly, how you can persuade them to engage with your company.

We hope the guide helps you along your journey to improved results from SEO. Please let us know what works best for you!

Dr Dave Chaffey has been involved "hands-on" in SEO since 1998 when he built his first site. Since then he has consulted and trained many marketers to help improve their results from search engine marketing, including representatives from 3M, BP, HSBC Commercial, Mercedes-Benz, Smith and Nephew and Sony Professional.

Dave is also author of five best-selling business books including Internet Marketing: Strategy, Implementation and Practice; and, Marketing eXcellence (with PR Smith).

Phil Robinson is an online marketing consultant with over 16 years experience in marketing planning, internet strategy and online acquisition.

In 2004, Phil founded ClickThrough, a ethical search marketing agency specialising in pay per click, online PR, SEO, social media and conversion optimisation. He gives best practice training for businesses, runs seminars and writes eBooks on digital marketing strategy.

Lindsey Annison is ClickThrough's chief blogger. A practising SEO consultant since 1996, Lindsey helps companies improve their website marketing, online PR and information architecture. Lindsey is also a qualified adult education lecturer and author.

As co-founder of the Access to Broadband Campaign, she has been instrumental in the provision of high-speed internet access to rural areas in the UK. Lindsey is also a past winner of Silicon.com's "Outstanding Contribution to UK Technology"

ClickThrough
the search conversion experts

ClickThrough is an international search marketing and conversion optimisation consultancy. Since 2004 we have helped our clients in the UK, USA and Europe reach new customers in over 30 countries, using our proven, ethical search marketing know-how. We pride ourselves on giving honest, actionable advice without up-front commitments:

- ✓ No contract tie-ins for clients, giving you peace of mind.
- ✓ We link the remuneration of our people to client goals.
- ✓ Modular service offerings means we can be as flexible as you need.
- ✓ Proven track record from our work in over 30 countries with clients including Peugeot, Vonage, Computeach, Norgren and DUO Boots.
- ✓ Our people all receive our industry-leading, Digital Academy training.
- ✓ Full account management team, with senior level contact for every client.
- ✓ Active members of the IAB, eConsultancy and SEMPO.
- ✓ Thought leaders, giving clients the inside track on what matters in search before it happens

Whether you are thinking of changing your search or digital marketing agency, or just looking to improve your online conversion rate, our team of search conversion experts can help.

Find out what we can do to grow your business. Call us on **0800 088 7486** or visit
www.clickthrough-marketing.com

What you will learn in this guide

ClickThrough
the search conversion experts

Introduction to...
Search Engine Optimisation

#1 Organic vs. Paid Search

In order to understand SEO, it's crucial to understand the difference between paid and organic search results. Fire up your web browser, bring up your favourite search engine and type in a popular search term e.g. "car insurance". Look at the SERPS (search engine results pages) that the search engine returns; you will see that some links at the top or side of the page are labeled 'Sponsored Links'. These placements are paid for by Advertisers. The other main list of results are unpaid listings, also called "organic search results", and it is these that SEO practitioners concern themselves with.

Many people prefer organic search results, possibly because of the reduction in hard sell. However, achieving top organic search results, especially in a competitive niche, is difficult. Nevertheless, if you have good, unique, keyword rich content on well constructed pages with multiple inbound links from authoritative sites, and regular updates, you stand a chance.

If you are prepared to put in the work and follow the tips and tricks in this guide, you can retain top positions for key terms for years.

#2 What is SEO?

SEO stands for Search Engine Optimisation. It is the process by which a website is prepared and optimised for the search engines so that maximum visibility and high rankings in organic search results are possible for that site. The term has become broader as the sector has developed, and much of what was originally known as SEO is now considered to be part of Internet Marketing (IM) or Search Engine Marketing (SEM).

Two main parts to SEO:
a) On-page optimisation
b) Off-page optimisation

The second is more commonly referred to now as SEM, but some still feel the terms are interchangeable and there are many areas of overlap. Many websites have been built with a view to design factors rather than SEO. However, only sites with the right SEO elements in place are likely to appear frequently in search results.

ClickThrough
the search conversion experts

#3 How Does SEO Differ From SEM?

Once you have optimised on-page, you need to begin working on bringing people to your website via diverse routes e.g. links on other sites or in forums, from articles, social media and so on. These are off-page marketing tactics, many of which are explored later in this guide, and are often referred to as part of SEM (Search Engine Marketing) or IM (Internet Marketing). SEO is different as it generally concerns itself with on-page factors. However, both need to be considered if you are to rank well.

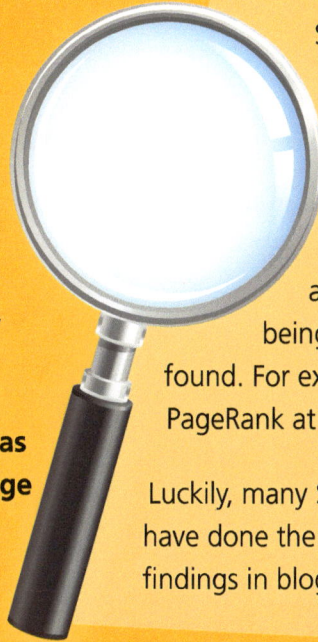

SEO is often considered a 'black art' because the actual algorithms the search engines use to decide where a website ranks for a particular search term or phrase are, in the main, unknown. However, with a little rooting around amongst patents, many of the technologies being used as well as the processes can be found. For example, you can find the first patent for PageRank at tinyurl.com/googlepatent.

Luckily, many SEO experts, like those at ClickThrough, have done the reading for you and summarized their findings in blog posts and guides like these.

Setting Out Your Goals

#4 Define Your Objectives Clearly

The main purpose of employing SEO and SEM techniques is, of course, to drive traffic to your website via multiple routes. Not just any traffic, but quality traffic. These are people who will be interested in your products, services and content, and are potential customers or clients.

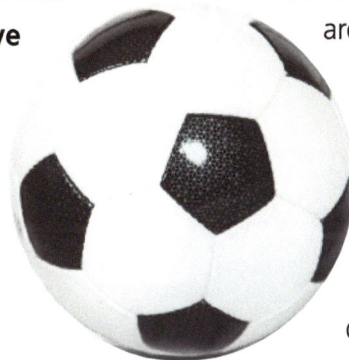

Define your objectives and goals clearly – what are you trying to achieve? Increased sales and enquiries, raising brand awareness, creating a mailing list, reducing marketing budget and getting a better ROI are all valid objectives. By defining goals, particularly as numeric targets or percentage increases, you can break your ambitions down into manageable, measurable chunks upon which to base your marketing plan .

ClickThrough
the search conversion experts

#5 Create Benchmarks Before Beginning

Before launching into applying the techniques in this guide, it is important to set benchmarks before you begin. In doing so, you are able to establish how applying SEO techniques has improved your sites performance. To do this analyse your existing traffic, conversion rates, and how much revenue your site is generating today.

Remember to make your goals achievable. "Being No 1 on the Search Engines" is too vague and out of your control. However, "Increase traffic by 15% over 3 months" is far more decisive and if you have known conversion rates e.g. number of sales from a certain number of visitors, you can assess the return on investment from your internet marketing activities. If you don't know your conversion rate, index.fireclick.com can give you an indication by sector, as can Google Analytics.

#6 Learning From Your Web Analytics

Now you have set your goals and defined benchmarks, you will need to measure them. Ever wondered how many people visit your site and how they got there? Wonder no more. Web analytics tools offer clear, in-depth information about potential customers visiting your site. You can use either a free package such as Google Analytics, getclicky.com or piwik.org, or a paid software application.

Your site stats are possibly the most valuable information you have about your website, and they are the key to maximizing the return from each visitor to your site. Before you start anything else, make the task of monitoring and analysing your site stats a priority in your online marketing routine. That way, you can track how you are progressing over time.

#7 Think About Visitor Journeys

Visitors to your site have come seeking specific information and it's important to make the journey to that information as short as possible. If information is not easily found from the page of entry, your visitors may ask "Are we nearly there yet?" one too many times and give up.

When designing your site, consider what information different types of visitors will be seeking, and make sure that whatever their end goal, the route will be concise and clear. Monitor visitor journeys through both your site stats and onsite search, and make changes where necessary.

Click Through
the search conversion experts

#8 The Benefits/Pitfalls of Buying a Domain

Search engines add a weighting for the age of a domain, depending on when it was first registered. The assumption is that if it is still around then the owner has shown enough interest to pay for the renewal of the domain each year.

When buying a second-hand domain you need to check its history. Has it ever been owned by an online fraudster, hosted inappropriate content, or been blacklisted by search engines?

Use archive.org to see how the site looked in the past, search for mentions of the old site, and proceed with caution. Is the domain name really that valuable to you if it could potentially be unusable?

However, if the domain is 'clean' and has relevant link weight then it could be a good investment. Once purchased, verify it in Google Webmaster tools. You can then use a 301 redirect to permanently pass the link weight to another site, if necessary.

Takeaways:

- Domain age carries search engine weight.

- Check the history of any domain you intend to buy.

- Consider the value of a second hand domain name vs. a brand new one.

#9 Keywords In Your Domain

For many years, the thinking was that your two, or at most three, major keywords needed to be in your domain name e.g. redrubberducks.co.uk. The use of hyphenation within the domain was also considered an issue – would search engines understand that the domain contained keywords?

Whilst it is believed that Bing and Google Caffeine give more weight to keyword phrases in your domain, you should only use keywords if they are relevant to your whole business, rather than one section of it.

Think about some of the biggest domain names there are; google.com, twitter.com, facebook.com – none include their major keywords of 'search engine', 'micro-blogging' or 'social network' in their names. They are brand names which are easy to remember, and have become part of everyday life. Try telling someone exactly how "wer2good2u.com" needs to be typed into the location bar! That said, your keywords should definitely be part of your URL structure.

#10 URL Structure

Although you may wish to avoid keywords in your domain, keywords should feature in the URL of each individual page. However, you should try to limit the number of keywords in your URL to between 3 and 5. This is for two reasons:

1. Shorter URLs are easier for site visitors to remember, and seem to be more attractive than very long URLS – hence the growth in the use of URL shortening services, such as **bit.ly**, **tinyurl.com** and **notlong.com**.

2. Too much information doesn't necessarily help the search engines weight your page accordingly. Keep those URLs short and sweet.

#11 Keywords Matter

It remains a constant surprise how many companies (or rather, their website designers) fail to realise the huge importance of keywords. Keywords are crucial; not just in optimisation for search engines and your PPC campaigns, but also in helping you communicate to site visitors using the words and phrases they would use themselves.

The most important thing you will ever have in your SEO armoury is your keyword list. Even a small company selling only a single product should have at least 500 words on that list. Remember that you should focus on long tail keywords (phrases containing multiple keywords) as well as top terms.

#12 Brainstorming Keywords

Selecting the right keywords is vital, and there are a number of ways to go about finding them:

- Read through all of your marketing material, product brochures, collateral and your website. What keywords stand out?

- Ask friends, family, colleagues and staff to suggest the words and phrases that relate to your business.

- Go online and check your competitors' sites for terms you may have missed.

- Use keyword suggestion tools such as **Wordtracker.com,** Google's Keyword Suggestion Tool, **keywordspy.com** and **seobook.com**.

- Look at the bottom of each Google search engine results page for alternative suggestions.

- Use visual search tools such as the Google Wonder Wheel, **quintura.com** and **kartoo.com** to suggest additional phrases you might not have thought of.

#13 Use Keywords Sensibly

Never forget that your website copy is there primarily to inform site visitors, rather than for search engines. Rather than including 50 keywords from your list in a single paragraph, use your keywords sparingly. Your copy still needs to make sense.

Group your keywords into subject areas, or themes, and use them within the right section of your site. This will help search engines understand what each page is about, and increase its ranking strength.

The relationship between a keyword and all other words on the page is called the keyword density. This is important to avoid your page being seen as spam by search engines. Although opinions differ, most SEO experts would recommend a density no higher than 3% for a specific word or phrase.

ClickThrough
the search conversion experts

#14 Long Tail Keywords

Over the last few years, the number of words in an average search phrase has risen from two to four or more. An example of a long tail term would be "last minute holiday Spain" where the initial search "last minute holiday" is being refined by adding additional words, in this case "Spain".

By using long tail terms in META tags, body copy and anchor text you can attract visitors to your site who are being more specific in their searches. These long tail searchers are not only self-qualifying as a potential target, but also helping you to whittle down the number of competitors that appear next to you on search results pages.

Find long tail keywords for your niche by using the Google Search Based Keyword tool to full effect (found at google.com/sktool). Start by simply entering your own website address. Then refine by search volume, before adding words to your keyword list.

#15 Forecasting Search Traffic

Your position in the search results will substantially affect the likelihood that your link will be clicked on. The Top 3 positions receive around two-thirds of the total clickthroughs for that search term, in ratios of approximately 42%, 12% and 8.5%. Interestingly, being at Number 10 i.e. last on Page 1 (2.3%) will generate fewer clickthroughs than being at Number 11 i.e. top of the Page 2 (4.3%).

You can use these figures to forecast how much traffic you can expect to receive. This will help you to judge the amount of time and resource needed to further optimise your site for specific terms. Increasing your position by even a few places in the organic SERPs can exponentially increase your traffic.

Creating Your Web Copy

#16 Getting Quality Content

Once you have you selected your target keywords you are ready to start thinking about your sites content. The copy, or text, on your page must reflect both your brand and the quality of your company, products and services. It also needs to communicate the key messages for your website.

Copy can have different purposes; to act as your sales pitch, to describe a product, or build your brand. Make sure that it does that job well. If you struggle to write copy, then hire a good copywriter. This can be inexpensive, and the right person will help you get your message across with precision.

ClickThrough
the search conversion experts

#17 Content is King

The content on your site should be fresh, original, informative, and valuable. This is one of the most important tips for your website. Content really is King. Search engines love quality, unique content and so do your visitors:

- Do not plagiarise content from others. There are too many ways to check e.g. copyscape.com.

- Archive everything so it will continue to bring search engine traffic for years to come.

- Should you charge for your content? Decide whether you want revenue from people paying for your content or whether you want to build a great free resource that your visitors recommend.

- Add content regularly. Are you going to a trade show? Having a sale? Put it on your site.

- Ask your visitors for ideas and inspiration for content. What do they want to know?

- Don't let your content go stale. Your company changes and evolves; so should your site.

- Keep up to date on industry news. Then write your take on it.

- This year's trend is...lists. Write a Top Ten or your own 101 Guide! Make it funny, instructive and helpful.

- Use secondary related keywords in your content to ensure that the search engines, and readers, are clear about the 'theme' of your copy.

#18 Spelling and Grammar

The speeling and grandmar used on yore websight kneads to bee perfect – no misteaks. Employ a good proofreader to check and double check for any errors you may have overlooked.

Many of the search engines now spellcheck searches (e.g. Did you mean this......?) so there is no need to deliberately include misspellings to capture people who struggle to spell certain words.

#19 Bridging Cultural Differences

There are many words which are spelt differently in US and UK English. Consider your audience. Cater for those you wish to deal with. There are instances where the difference in meanings can render a UK site a place of confusion to an American, and vice versa.

When translating into a foreign language, use translators that know the culture of the country that they are translating for, rather than just speaking the language. An honest mistake in translation can transform a simple sentence into something a native reader could find offensive. If your budget can't stretch to a full translation, offer the option for visitors to translate pages by linking to translate.google.com.

ClickThrough
the search conversion experts

#20 WIIFM

The first question a visitor will ask on arriving at your website is "What's In It For Me?", also known as WIIFM and pronounced "wiffim". Your aim is to answer that question as quickly and succinctly as possible for each and every visitor to your site.

This is why concise landing pages, easy site navigation, well-written copy and simple page layouts are so important. When a searcher types in their query to the search engines and clicks on your link, they want to be taken to a page that helps them find the answer or product they are seeking.

#22 Just Seven Seconds

Is all you have to convince your customers they are on the right website. Often people leave after a few seconds. Think carefully what questions they are asking and how you are going to provide the answers. Get into the mind of your site visitors. You can find out how long they spend each time they come to your site by using stats from your analytics or with reference to competitor sites using research tools such as Nielsen NetRatings or **Alexa.com**.

#21 Only One Click Away

Never forget that the rest of the Web, including all of your competitors' websites, is just one click away. Look after and nurture your site visitors and they will give attention and time back. By answering the WIIFM question as soon as possible, you will help them to clearly understand why they are on your website, and with easy navigation, you can lead them to the product, service or solution they seek.

#23 Providing Access For All

In some countries, there are now laws concerning the accessibility of commercial and public sector websites for those with disabilities. For example, people with a visual impairment can use a screen reader to access websites. Check the law to see whether your site complies. In the UK, the Royal National Institute of the Blind can offer advice about how the Disability Discrimination Act 2005 may apply to you (see **http://tinyurl.com/disabilityuk**).

ClickThrough
the search conversion experts

#24

Copy Isn´t Just For Search Engines

Your website copy must answer the WIIFM question for your visitors, offer informative and unique content, and act as your sales rep, shop window and helpline.

Many people have fallen into the trap over the years of trying to write copy wholly for the search engines, rather than considering the visitors to the website. Search engines will not buy your products, talk about your site to friends, family and colleagues, rave about you in their blog, or print out coupons and spend them in your shop.

#25

Crafting Your Page Layout

You would not employ a plumber to fix your television, so don't expect a graphic designer to understand how your website should be constructed. A website is navigated and read in a very different way to a book or magazine. Your visitors will use different sized monitors, in **small**, **medium**, **large fonts**, with images switched on or off.

You should always make pages very simple to read, rather than text heavy. Keep text in small blocks, use headlines to give a quick taster of the subject matter, employ images to break up the text, and use plenty of white space which keeps the page clean. Design should never take priority over usability.

ClickThrough
the search conversion experts

#26 The Perfect Landing Page

The purpose of a good landing page is to direct visitors arriving through a search engine directly to information related to their search query. Landing pages should also incorporate a 'call to action' e.g. a quote request form, newsletter signup box, white paper download link, or the ability to purchase a product directly from the page.

Landing pages should take into account the differences between visitors from PPC (Pay Per Click) ads, and organic search results. Keyword rich content on landing pages written with SEO in mind can also increase the quality score of your PPC campaign.

Where a landing page is used for both paid and organic search the general rule of thumb is that PPC content is 'above the fold', and SEO content 'below the fold' (or the content you can only see when you scroll downwards).

Keep your landing pages simple, and make sure that all traffic to the page is monitored to ensure that it is delivering the results you require, and not turning people away. It's important to strike a balance between optimising for conversion, and creating a cul-de-sac where it is difficult for visitors to navigate to other areas of your site.

Takeaways:

1. **Landing pages work for both organic search results and PPC.**
2. **Make your landing pages highly relevant to the visitors original search.**
3. **Keep calls to action simple and measurable.**

#27 Using H1, H2 <Tags>

Search engines assume that you will use your H1 and heading tags to display valuable information to your visitor. They also assume that text that appears in italics, bold or has been underlined, is important as is the convention in print.

For this reason, your headers and those items that are in bold, italics, or underlined, should contain your most important keywords to convey to both visitors and search engines alike that you consider this information to be important

#28 To META or Not To META

Meta tags provide information within the <HEAD> tags of a webpage which can help search engines categorize them. These are embedded in the pages HTML and are not visible to site visitors. They include description, keyword and title tags. META tags should be included on each page of a website, and should be tailored to each page. Although there is some debate as to the importance of META tags, you should always include keyword and title tags for basic SEO.

ClickThrough
the search conversion experts

HTML Validation

In the same way that you check your text for spelling, the code behind your site also needs to be error-free. There are many free HTML validators available (e.g. **validator.W3.org**) and you should make sure that your site meets all the required standards so it can be rendered accurately by as many browsers as possible.

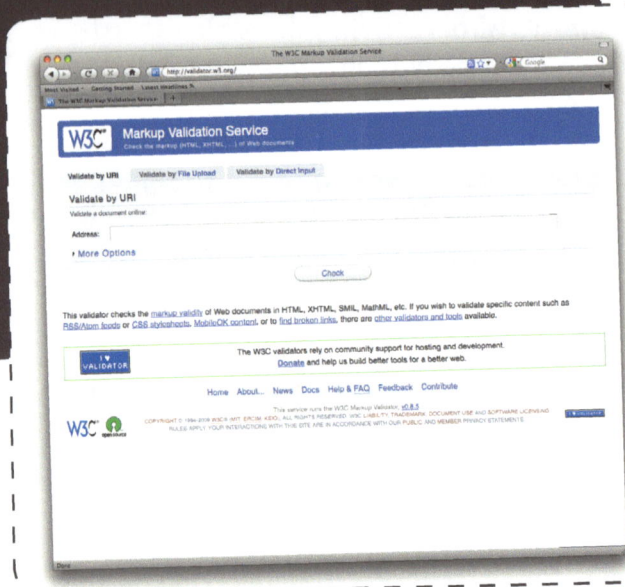

Make Page Titles Count

Your page titles should include the most important keywords for that page, as well as being descriptive. The title tag is reproduced at the top of most browsers and quickly summarises the page content to the user. Do not be tempted to use the page title 'Homepage', or 'About Us'.

Instead put your company name, or use your keywords in the title: 'Internet Marketing Services | Search Engine Optimisation'. Note the pipe character | gives clear results in the SERPs, and is proven to be better for clickthrough rates.

ClickThrough
the search conversion experts

#31 Why You Must Use Images

Images can break a page up, display a product and make copy easier to read by illustrating key messages. Image sizes should be relatively small to improve page load, and yet optimised to give the best onscreen resolution. When appropriate, use thumbnails with the option to see a larger image when clicked on.

Always put a descriptive alt img tag on every single image. This helps with Access for All (for blind and disabled users), and also give search engines what they need to understand

#32

Optimising Images

Images are an increasingly important resource for search engines to index. As early as Aug 2007, Omni Marketing Interactive were reporting that 16% of all web searches were for images, and that has grown to around a quarter of all online searches today.

Competition within image search is fierce, with numerous sites targeting keywords. As an example of how many new images are being added, look at the change in top results for the term 'Mona Lisa' over a 6 week period at **tinyurl.com/monalisadance.**

There are four important considerations for image optimisation.

1. File names should not be generic e.g. 'image1.jpg' but a name relevant to the image content e.g. 'online-pr-logo.jpg'.

2. Always put a descriptive alt img tag on every single image, not just for Access for All, but also to help the search engines understand why the image is relevant to your copy or the theme of that page.

3. Use tools such as **smush.it** to retain quality whilst reducing file size for a faster download time.

4. Make sure that the text in close proximity to the image on the page reinforces the image content by using appropriate keywords and tags.

#33 Latent Semantic Indexing

Seeking top rankings for highly competitive terms and phrases can be a lengthy process, and may actually yield less clickthroughs over time than optimising for secondary and related terms. "Latent semantic indexing" refers to the process that search engines are now using to determine the topic or theme of a page to then offer it as a relevant search result, although it may not directly include the actual search term.

This process views each document as a whole, and compares it with other documents, to see which words or terms are common to all. This is why it is becoming increasingly important to use related words, synonyms and alternative phrases to assist the search engines to define the content, and hence relevance, of your content to a specific search.

#35 Get Found With Site Maps

A site map can help both your website visitor and search engines. Visitors use them to quickly and easily navigate to specific pages that are deep within your site, or that they may have visited previously but failed to bookmark.

Search engines also use site maps as a starting point when reading your website. An XML Sitemap should be created; this can be verified in Google, Yahoo and Bing webmaster tools. This gives search engines a clear understanding of your site structure and priority pages. You can now also add site maps of your multimedia and video content to your search engine listing.

#34

A Simple Matter of Redirection

Be careful when moving your website to a new domain, and when you change the architecture of your site with a re-design. Links to the old address will now instead take visitors to 404 pages or Page Not Found. Rather than trying to get every person who has ever linked to you to change to the new versions, use 301 redirects on all the old URLs to point to the new site. For large sites, you may need to seek the help of a programmer so that the process of creating redirects can be automated. Even on a small site it can be a slow process, but it is always going to be worthwhile.

The page cannot be found

The page you are looking for might have been removed, had its name changed, or is temporarily unavailable.

Please try the following:

- Make sure that the Web site address displayed in the address bar of your browser is spelled and formatted correctly.
- If you reached this page by clicking a link, contact the Web site administrator to alert them that the link is incorrectly formatted.
- Click the Back button to try another link.

HTTP Error 404 - File or directory not found.
Internet Information Services (IIS)

Technical Information (for support personnel)

- Go to Microsoft Product Support Services and perform a title search for the words **HTTP** and **404.**
- Open **IIS Help**, which is accessible in IIS Manager (inetmgr), and search for topics titled **Web Site Setup, Common Administrative Tasks,** and **About Custom Error Messages.**

Click Through
the search conversion experts

#36
Incy Wincy Spider

Have you ever wondered how the search engines find and read your site? They use a spider, which is an automated program, or bot, which crawls the Web, indexing websites. Then, using complex algorithms, the search engines assign your website a ranking in the results pages for specific key phrases.

You should let the spiders in! However, you should restrict access to areas of your website for which you charge, or you will find your premium content listed for all to see, for free. This is done by the use of NOFOLLOW and NOINDEX tags and your Robots.txt.

#37 How Search Engines See Your Site

A search engine spider will not see your website as a human does. It cannot tell that an image on your page is of a football, unless you have included an image ALT tag which tells it so. If a link does not lead to the page you intended and instead leads to a 404 or Page Not Found, the spider will not endeavour to find the right link. Spiders are not that keen on many of the new technologies e.g. Javascript and Flash, and they are not at all keen on the use of frames.

If you want to know how your site appears to a search engine, try the spider simulator tools at **tinyurl.com/spidertools.**

#38 What is Readable Text?

Search engines work on the principle that if they can see something, your site visitors should also be able to see it. For this reason, readable text is also indexable text.

You can find what text is readable on your website simply by putting the mouse at the top left of the browser window, clicking the left mouse button, and dragging the cursor to the bottom right. Everything that is highlighted is readable text.

Check it for keywords, spelling and grammar, to reassure yourself that the copy achieves its purpose, and to make sure the search engines really do have something to work with!

#39 Query Demands Freshness

'Query demands freshness', or QDF, is an important mantra to repeat often. Your website content should be regularly updated using a dynamic content platform, such as a blog or RSS feed. Search engines value new content, as do your visitors. Check your older content – if it out of date, and is not bringing in traffic, update it or replace it with fresh content. Don't remove entire pages because they could be still bringing in 'long tail' traffic. Instead use a 301 or 302 to redirect that traffic to newer content.

#40 Watch The Time

There are multiple factors which will affect your site's SEO that are more technical. For instance, increasingly, Google is taking note of page load time by giving pages a 'load time grade'. Check the page load of your site by logging into or creating your Google Adwords account or or by running your site through **http://tinyurl.com/yahooslow.**

Page load will also affect your visitors – a page which takes an age to appear on the screen is a frequent cause of visitors leaving a website.

#41 All About PageRank?

PageRank used to be one of the most important factors in SEO. Google introduced it in 1998 to help eliminate spam within search results. For many site owners, gaining a high PageRank was a key monitor of success, as it helped them swap quality links from similarly ranked sites.

However, in October 2009, Google admitted that PageRank was no longer included in their webmaster tools, after years of being subjected to spam and hijacking attempts. PageRank has been an indication of authority when link building, but equally as important is the age of the domain, likely site visitors, and quality of the content on the site. The message today is that you shouldn't worry overly about PageRank.

#42 Using Micro-formats and Metadata

Meta data is information for the search engines which is hidden within the code of the site. This information is increasingly being used to add new functionality into search and PPC, to help improve the relevancy of rankings, and the information available to searchers.

Your meta data includes not just keywords, title, description, and author; one of the new additions to this area is the addition of contact information which can appear in a search listing.

At the start of 2010, this is being used as a beta feature for showing the contact details of the top ranking sites using PPC, but it is likely that this will be extended in the future.

#43 Don't Forget Yahoo! and Bing

Whilst many SEO agencies and practitioners tend to focus on Google, who have around 90% of the market, it is worth remembering that the remaining 10% can bring in substantial traffic too.

Optimise your site for Yahoo! and Bing. Both have advantages e.g. Bing is known for having a powerful image search interface, and Yahoo! for allowing easy filtering of results from authoritative sources. The recent paid search alliance between the two engines may mean more commonality between their search technologies in future. There are other engines which take 1% or less of search traffic, but your priorities should be the three major engines.

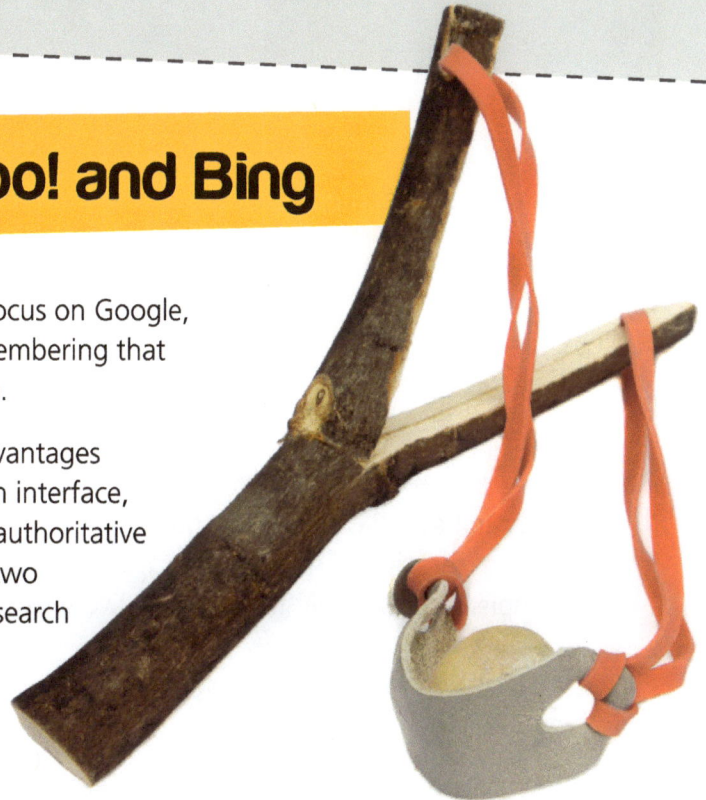

#44 Think Beyond the Search Engines

Whilst many SEO agencies only offer SEO and SEM services, that ignores the fact that your potential target audience spends most of their time away from the search engines. Your audience also use forums, socialise on social networks, send tweets, write blog posts, follow links, read articles, check their emails, use the mobile web, watch videos, listen to podcasts, and much, much more.

Find out where, and how, your audience spends time online. Then, communicate with them using the methods they prefer, and you will start to attract quality traffic to your website.

#45 Links: Search Lifeblood

Links are the lifeblood that power the strength of your website in SERPs. Here's what you need to know about them:

You can never have too many good links, especially if you source links from complementary, rather than competitive sites.

Check all your existing links and anchor text are optimised.

Create a link from your own site to another person's site, before requesting one back.

Suggest the right place for your link, which shows the webmaster you have taken the time to look at their site.

Help your visitors link to you by offering a range of banner creatives, and linking instructions.

Add social bookmarks tools, e.g. addthis.com, to your site. They help visitors add your site to their social bookmarking account (e.g. digg.com, stumbleupon.com and del.icio.us - an online version of the favorites folder which allows you to share bookmarks with others). This will create another link to your content and site.

Building

Submit your site to industry and geographic directories, as well as to large, authoritative sites directories such as **dmoz.org** and **dir.yahoo.com**.

Use trackbacks and pingbacks to track links to your blog.

Create permalinks (permanent links to each posting) for your blog.

Keep track of your links, and thank people for linking to you. They will be more likely to link again!

Find places to submit links to your site by using the appropriate search syntax, within the search engines e.g. your keyword + "addurl", or "Suggest link"

If you have a blog, submit to blog directories.

Similarly, if you have an RSS feed, remember to add it to RSS feed directories.

Think carefully before buying links. Whilst paying for inclusion in an industry directory is one thing, bribing a blogger to feature a rave review of your product may do more harm than good.

Check regularly for linkrot and remove non-working links.

Find everywhere you can to be listed, but remember quality beats quantity every time.

But most important – create stand out content, tools and services that other site owners will naturally want to link to because they are valuable and entertaining for their audiences.

#46 Controlling Link Velocity

How quickly do other sites link to your new content or new pages? This is an important consideration as spam sites tend to amass links very quickly using a range of black hat techniques, and search engines hate spam. By building links quickly, spammers can move their sites to the top of the SERPS on the back of their supposed popularity. In reality, spammers use multiple accounts on social networks and bookmarking sites, with automated link building, to fool the search engines.

Increase link velocity by applying similar techniques, but in a manual, ethical manner. When you add a new blog post, add it to Twitter, social bookmark sites, social networks and so on. This way, you can reach a far wider audience who will then link to your content and give your link velocity rating a boost, without the risk of getting banned.

#47 Targeting Your Anchor Text

Anchor text is the portion of text on a page, typically one or two words, that you have formatted as a link to another site or page. Anchor text must be relevant to the content of the page being linked to. For instance, *Click here* will not gain you any brownie points from either the search engines or your visitors because it is neither descriptive nor informative. Think carefully about what to use as your anchor text when writing your copy because well-used anchor text can be worth its weight in search engine gold.

#48 Watch Who You Link To

Link to established and reputable sites only, where at all possible.
Do a little research, seek out reviews of the sites in question, check who else links to them and how respected those sites are. Search engines and visitors will trust your site more if they recognize and respect the sites you link to.

ClickThrough
the search conversion experts

Best Practice

In order to drive visitors around your own site, rather than lose them to another website, you should create internal links to lead your visitors to related articles, similar products, and additional content. These will engage visitors with your brand which means that they are more likely to search for you by brand next time – and it's much easier to rank highly for terms containing your brand name

Your anchor text must be relevant and contain keywords. Cross link as many pages as you can, but only where relevant. Link to pages which are deep within your site from top level and category pages. Find the pages with many external links pointing to them and cross-link internally to these. You can do this by typing: link: "http://www.mysite.com/specific-page-URL -site:mysite.com into Google, where 'mysite.com' is your own URL.

#50 Checking Link Age

You should regularly check that all your links are still valid, and not suffering from link rot. Link rot is when a link no longer points to the intended content, and instead reaches a 404 (a non-existent page or one that has moved). Worse still, if that domain that has transferred ownership it may now include irrelevant or inappropriate content.

Use google.com/webmasters/tools to find broken links, and all the backlinks that Google can see. Check your links biannually. If you find broken links they can be resolved by contacting the webmasters of sites which link to you.

ROAD ENDS

ClickThrough
the search conversion experts

#51 Why Should Visitors Trust You?

This is a rarely mentioned, but strategic element of optimisation. As a business, one of your primary concerns is to establish trust with your customers. As a website, you need to apply similar thinking in order to succeed with the search engines, who put a considerable weight on 'trust'.

For your customers, include industry accreditation logos, security verification certificates, full contact details, and testimonials. For the search engines, make sure your links point to and from reputable sources, that your content is unique, and follow all of the search engines' own guidelines and rules. The use of all of these elements will help your visitors feel more at ease with your site and, by extension, your brand.

#52 First Contact

Make sure all your contact details are up to date and very easy to find on your website. Customers and search engines need to be convinced that you really do exist! The lack of a telephone number, a P.O. Box address, or just an email contact point automatically generates a level of concern in the customer's mind.

Adding your full postal address will also help you feature in local searches for your geographic area.

#53 Work Online As You Do Offline?

Reputation management is becoming a key concern of many online businesses, who fear negative reviews on forums or consumer backlash websites. Yet many incidents can be avoided if you apply the same honesty that you display offline, online. Network with those who you feel will be of value to your business and website; give generously and without necessarily seeking an instant return; steer away from the hard sell; and establish yourself as a genuine and honest company who people wish to deal with. They are key factors in helping to build a reputation for fair dealing, online.

#54 People Power Shaping SERPs

Look up how TrustRank and Yahoo! HarmonyRank are being used to ensure that spammy pages which beat the search engine algorithms are being weeded out by real people. These methods are likely to be increasingly used to combat spam in the SERPs, and are built on sound philosophies about trust amongst humans and businesses. By working ethically in your SEO and business practices, you stand to benefit from the use of consumer opinion in search algorithms.

ClickThrough
the search conversion experts

#55 SEO No Gos

Do not use unethical techniques, also known as 'black hat' tactics. These can result in lower rankings and even get your website banned by the search engines. To double check whether something you are planning is the right thing to do, ask in an SEO forum or run a quick search.

Here are some of the most common techniques that you should avoid at all costs:

- Putting as many keywords onto a page as possible, known as keyword stuffing.
- Using popular search terms which are irrelevant to your site purely to pull in traffic.
- Using invisible text e.g. making text he same colour as the background.
- Hiding text behind images so only search engines can see it, not visitors.
- Duplicating content on multiple domains for no reason except to mislead search engines.

- Presenting a different version of a page to a search engine spider than that seen by human visitors aka cloaking.
- Using an automated program aka screenscraper to steal high ranking content from other sites and put it on your own.
- Using link farms (chains of low quality scraped sites) to create hundreds of visible and hidden links back to your site, known as link spam.

Inside Your Customers Mind

#56 Think As Your Customers Think

In order to best serve your customers online, you need to understand who they are, and how they think..

Creating profiles, or personas, for each type of visitor/customer who visits your site will help you immediately generate powerful insights, including what they are looking for from your site. Examples of online personas can be found at **http://tinyurl.com/personas1** and **http://tinyurl.com/personas2**.

Get into the minds of your visitor, and see your company and website as they do. Make the required changes so that your customers are happy customers who will recommend you to others.

ClickThrough
the search conversion experts

#57 Securing Visitor Feedback

When seeking information from your site visitors, try not to be pushy. When asking visitors for feedback make it clear what information you are looking for. Do you want their opinion on a new site design, your latest ad creative or the quality of your customer service? Tell them what you want to know..

How to get feedback:

- ✓ Polls.
- ✓ Surveys.
- ✓ Pop up windows.
- ✓ Through social networks.
- ✓ Feedback forms.
- ✓ Discussion and focus groups.
- ✓ Customer feedback sites e.g. getsatisfaction.com.

After receiving feedback send a prompt reply, and answer specific points in person rather than using an automated response. Then, aggregate all feedback so that it can be easily referred to by those within your company who need to hear it. Customer feedback can form the basis of your Frequently Asked Questions, and act as an ongoing mandate for decisions you have made on the back of previous feedback.

Takeaways

- Be clear about what feedback you are seeking from your audience.
- Respond personally where possible.
- Make use of the valuable feedback you are given.

ClickThrough
the search conversion experts

#58 Conducting Market Research

Want to know what your online customers think in depth? Conducting online market research need not be expensive. There are some very simple tools to survey your customers, e.g. surveymonkey.com and questionpro.com as well as services such as brainjuicer.com with panels of people you can question.

Decide what it is you need to know from the research, set a budget, and seek the right tools for the job. For example you could create a ning.com group to quickly build an impromptu focus group, use a free tool to quickly create a survey on your website, and add Live Help to your site so that your customers can interact with you directly. You could also think about using Google Trends to track fluctuations in search volumes for specific phrases, and use trendistic.com to keep an eye on what's hot on Twitter in your field of interest.

#59 Getting To Know Your Audience Better

If you need more detailed data on your audience's behaviour and demographics, as well as your competitors' sites, you can make use of the following:

Google AdPlanner and Quantcast are free tools that will help you find the sites where your audience are most likely to be found. Hitwise have access to possibly the largest data set about user behaviour for profiling and identifying your key target audience. Whilst not cheap, the data can reveal fascinating insights for your business. Read 'Click' by Bill Tancer to get the inside story on using Hitwise data
http://tinyurl.com/clickbilltancer

#60 Centre of Your Audience's World

Regularly seek out new content that will be of interest to your target audience and link to it. Especially if it has been in the news or has gone viral. Be topical. Become the source of aggregated news for your industry sector, and audience, by pooling together all the news feeds from your industry into one place.

Find the latest news by keeping an eye on hashtags (#) for your sector on Twitter (#77 – hashtags are used to identify posts on a particular topic e.g. #digitalbritain), through RSS feeds from blogs with a small yet niche audience, or from online industry specific publications.

#61 Syndicate Your Content

Letting other people use your content can be highly beneficial. Whether this is through an RSS feed or by creating syndication deals, it will lead to a wider audience. There are multiple types of content you can syndicate, from white papers, to articles, to blog posts, news and thought leadership pieces. Don't be shy in sharing! It will lead to more people finding out about your site.

#62 PPC Advertising

Pay Per Click or PPC is the method by which website owners can pay to advertise on search engines for specific phrases. PPC listings on third party sites can be indexed, and campaigns can have a small amount of SEO benefit. PPC is complex subject and before planning a PPC campaign you should fully investigate your competition, the likely budget needed, and have an expert plan and manage your campaign. If you find you need help, ClickThrough employs a number of Google AdWords Professionals who can design a bespoke PPC campaign around your needs and targets.

#63 Harnessing Twitter To Fuel Your Marketing

If you haven't discovered Twitter, you really should try it. From a marketing perspective, it has many uses. Firstly, news is currently breaking faster on Twitter faster than any other medium. If something is going to go viral, that activity will begin on Twitter first.

Secondly, as you gather followers, you will find that the links in your tweets that direct back to your site are clicked on more frequently. Your followers will then share (retweet or RT) these links to their circle of followers if they like the content, and so on.

Twitter is also a great place for 'people watching', whether that is your competitors or your audience. You can also follow hashtags (#), which relate to specific topics of interest to you e.g. industry conferences, events or news for your sector.

Today, go to Twitter and grab your company's Twitter username before someone else does!

#64 Find Your Audience on Social Networks

Some marketers still believe that social networks are a waste of time for people who only want to tell you what they had for lunch. In reality, it is where huge sections of the population are conducting their personal and professional lives. In 2009 more people communicated using Facebook than web based email.

It is important to choose the social networks used by your audience. For industry connections, use **linkedin.com**, **xing.com** and **ecademy.com**, both for your company and key individuals. Be warned though before adding all of your staff – recruiters headhunt using these sites.

To gain consumer visibility, look to create a Facebook fan page, or if you are more ambitious use **ning.com** to create your own social network. There are plenty of other social networks to reach specific geographic, age or interest demographics e.g. **odnoklassniki.ru** (a Russian social network), **eons.com** (baby boomer social network) and **deviantart.com** (art-based social network).

Takeaways:

1. Social networks are already of great importance.
2. Locate the social networks used by your audience .
3. Participate and be social.

#65 Get Your Products on Google Base

Search engines have realised the power of having multiple different types of results e.g. video, maps and real-time news. That has prompted a rise in shopping results woven into the SERPs. Are your products listed? They should be if you want to reach people who are looking to buy the exact product that you sell.

Getting listed in Google Merchant Center is easy, even if you have thousands of products. However, there are certain criteria you need to meet before your optimised XML feed is accepted for inclusion. For instance, each product must be listed on its own page on your website. Don't delay, get listed today!

ClickThrough
the search conversion experts

#66 E-commerce and Comparison Directories

Many consumers now search comparison sites to find the best deal for the product they are seeking, and read reviews of products from satisfied (and dissatisfied) customers to help make a purchase decision.

List your products on **kelkoo.co.uk**, **uk.shopping.com** and encourage customers to write reviews of your products on sites such as **reviewcentre.com** and **revoo.com**.

#67 Effective Forum Marketing

Forums are great places to learn, gather feedback, and share your expertise. Posting useful information in forums (as well as Yahoo! Answers, answers.com, and industry specific answers sites e.g. LinkedIn discussion groups) can help you gain reputation points, create links to your site, build brand recognition, and conduct market research about what your audience are looking for.

Always check the forum rules before posting and remember to lurk (or 'look') before you post to get a measure of the audience. When you are ready to post complete your profile information with a logo, photo or avatar; your company details and URL, and a sig (signature file) if it is permitted. Most of all, be friendly and helpful at all times.

wiki, wiki, WOW

#68

There are numerous 'wikis' on the Internet, which depend on user contributions for accuracy and depth of content.

The most famous is **wikipedia.org**, but many more exist. You can become a contributor, and add content, based on your experience and knowledge, which will raise awareness of you as an individual or your company.

You can find wikis on specific subjects by taking a Wiki Tour Bus and exploring the many interlinked wikis available:
http://meatballwiki.org/wiki/TourBusMap

ClickThrough
the search conversion experts

#69

The Importance of Brands

Your brand is one of the most important assets that you own, and building a reputable, quality, consistent and trustworthy brand should be of long-term importance to you.

There are many ways of building your brand, and we have already touched on many of these in this guide already. Choose the strategies for which you can commit sufficient resources to have a positive effect over a period of time. Never lose site of your core brand identity, and make sure the messages that are key to you are consistently delivered to your target audience.

#70 Get Blogging

Blogging has multiple benefits, both for SEO, and in brand building. Site visitors love interesting content, and posting regularly can help you grow a community of regularly returning readers who want your take on events and news. Search engines also love blogs as they provide timely, and fresh, content to index, and adding tags to your blog to help them is essential

Blog posts need not be lengthy, but they should encourage readers to comment, debate and link. For those reasons, don't be afraid to be opinionated, take novel approaches to subjects, and when someone comments on your blog, show you care by responding.

Before you jump right in, bear in mind that you will need to post regularly; visitors shouldn't find tumbleweed blowing across the deserted screenscape of your blog when they arrive!

Takeaways:

1. **Pick a subject or theme for your blog, and stick to it.**
2. **Post regularly and enthusiastically.**
3. **Encourage interaction.**

#71 No Budget?

Think Guerrilla Marketing

Surprisingly, many companies fail to apply any guerrilla marketing techniques; instead, playing the traditional, conformist game and therefore not standing out from their competitors.

It is impossible to list all the ways in which you can use guerrilla marketing, but here are a few examples for different types of businesses:

- Set up 404 pages (Page Not Found) with a mischievous, humorous tone. You will be amazed at how many people will link to them.

- Set up a Facebook or LinkedIn group, and/or ning.com network for your likely customers, centred around a subject that you know will interest them.

- Use Google's Sidewiki to put comments on other websites whose target audience might use your services and visit your website.

Guerrilla marketing strategies are unconventional, surprising, unexpected and thought-provoking, and yet should still re-inforce your key messages. Most importantly, guerrilla marketing should be low budget, but not low key.

Takeaways:

1. **Think out of the box.**
2. **The limit is your imagination, not your budget.**
3. **Ensure that your message is not lost along the way.**

The Daily Times

TUESDAY

BIG NEWS!

Crafting Press Releases

Press releases are as important today for online marketing as they have ever been. Getting in the habit of sending out regular press releases will help you promote your business and improve your SEO performance by gaining additional backlinks. PR is no longer just about mainstream media; you should be targeting multiple websites, news agencies and bloggers, to ensure your message reaches your niche audience.

Try to think like a publisher when writing press releases. What would you find interesting enough to put on your website? When you have written the perfect release, press release submission services, such as **PRWeb.com**, **PRNewsWire.com**, **BusinessWire.co.uk**, and **OnlinePRNews.com** can get your message out quickly.

As well as publishing the press release on their own site they will add it to their RSS feeds, post it to Twitter, and make it available to journalists and publications. You should also find the appropriate person within each publication within your industry to whom you can submit press releases directly.

#73 Creating Your Company Newsletter

An email newsletter should be an integral part of every company, large or small. The gift of a receptive customer is not one to be squandered.

Make your newsletters informative, with a balance between sales promotion, and industry insight. Short emails, with links leading back to your sites content with a taster summary, are in order. Archive your newsletters on your website to create an additional resource.

It is important that all email correspondence such as newsletters, is 'double opt-in'. This means that the subscriber receives an email which contains a link, so that they can confirm that they do wish to receive the newsletter.

Click.Through
the search conversion experts

#74 Using Autoresponders Effectively

Why make life difficult for yourself when you can automate so many tasks these days?

Smart autoresponders will allow you to send a series of emails to your subscribers and customers and provide, detailed data about open rates, conversions and unsubscribes. You can also use the data to run some multi-variate and A/B testing of sales copy and images.

By using the timeshift capability of autoresponders imaginatively you can deliver a full training course over a series of weeks or every chapter of a book in sequence. You can also reduce admin by sending an immediate holding email when an enquiry arrives, or to distribute product information sheets to enquirers.

#75 The Power of Article Marketing

Writing articles is a fantastic way to show your expertise on a subject, but make sure it is your knowledge you are sharing.

DON'T COPY COPY

Archive all of your articles on your website so that they can be indexed for long tail search traffic, and research the best sites to submit your articles to in order to gain a wider readership. The most well-known and reputable sites include **ezinearticles.com**, **goarticles.com**, and **iSnare.com**. Remember to post a link to your article on Twitter with a snappy headline, and never refuse an offer to write guest articles for well-respected or authoritative websites.

Content Beyond Text

#76 Hook Your Visitors With Downloads

Whether it is a podcast, a video, an ebook or a white paper, offering free downloads to your visitors helps to engage with them, and share information. In return for a download, you can ask in return for an email address and name. Asking people to complete lengthy forms is a turn off, and you will lose more people than you gain. To increase form completion, explain that you need their information to be able to send them a link to the download.

After a few days you can send a follow-up email about the product referred to, or to request feedback and their opinion on the download. Never spam their address, and never sell or share the addresses with a third party. You will be able to see the popularity of all downloads you offer in your web analytics package.

#77 Harnessing Videos and Podcasts

With the growth in sales of smartphones and iPhones, and the increase in broadband takeup, videos and podcasts have become a highly engaging way of sharing content with your target audience.

Search engines love non-text based content. In June 2009, there were 3.6 billion search queries about videos, 27% of all Google searches. Google now often incorporates video results on the first page of results, so having a library of video content can assist in stealing top listings from your competitors.

The best videos and podcasts are not hard-sell, but instead offer viewers something useful e.g. a step-by-step 'how to', the use of comedy, or a hands-on product review.

Listing your audio visual content on sites such as youtube.com, metacafe.com, dailymotion.com and podcastdirectory.com, and using relevant tags and keywords will also help to increase your rankings.

Takeaways:

1. Video and audio content offers a more engaging way of connecting with your audience.
2. Video results can occur in the first page of search engine results.
3. Make your videos useful to the audience to get the best response.

Holding On To Your Visitors

#78 Keep Track Of Your Visitors

Now you have your content in place, learn all you can about your visitors' habits on your website so that you can benefit from the knowledge.

Make sure you know:

a) How your visitors found you and monitor your referrals.

b) Which are the most and least popular pages on your site, and why.

c) How long people spend on your site.

d) Why people leave your site.

e) Which calls to action are converting most/least effectively.

There are multiple other uses of your site stats so spend time getting to know all the features of your analytics package.

ClickThrough
the search conversion experts

#79 No Website Usability, No Sales

Your website needs to work in all the major browsers, on different sized monitors, be accessible to those with colour blindness or who use a screen reader and so on. In every instance, it needs to remain as easy to use as possible. If you ignore website usability practice then you run the risk of ending up with an unusable site.

The most famous example of how a simple design change can affect your website usability profitability is the true story of the $300 Million Button written about by Jared M. Spool. Jared discovered a major fault within the online purchase process of the huge online retailer he worked for; after adding a product to their basket visitors were asked to either login, or register. He found that the majority of shoppers abandoned their visit at this point. Removing this hurdle made the company $300 million in addition sales in the first year.

Whilst your website may not suffer from such acute losses because of a website usability issue, it is likely that there are some usability issues on your site you may not be aware of. Regular testing and seeking feedback from visitors will help you to identify and solve such issues. For example, when planning your sites information architecture strive to structure your content so that visitors are led to the information they seek as easily as possible.

Simple changes such as the text on a button, or even the colour of an icon can affect how visitors react. By using Google Optimizer you will be able to test different headlines, buttons and landing pages before making large changes. When in doubt, **KISS** (**K**eep **I**t **S**imple **S**tupid). Your website should aim to be simple rather than deliberately complex. Unnecessary choices should be minimalised and paths through your website straightforward.

You can find out how the majority of visitors to your site will respond to changes by conducting user testing first. You only need a small yet representative group to run a robust test. Find 5 or 6 people, sit them in front of your website and watch. Alternatively, use a click tracking service such as **clicktale.com** or **crazyegg.com** to see what your visitors are doing.

You can also learn a lot about your sites usability from your web analytics tool.
Do you have pages with high exit or 'bounce' rates? Why are people leaving from those pages? Give careful consideration to any such pages and test changes to prevent people leaving prematurely.

Takeaways:

1. **Regularly confirm that your site is usable and working for your visitors, the search engines and you.**
2. **Test, evaluate and monitor the usability of your site regularly.**
3. **Do not be scared of making changes to your site if they follow usability best practice.**

#80 Encourage Return Visitors

Loyal customers are of immense value to your business, and one of your key priorities should be to encourage return visitors to your website. This means keeping in touch with them regularly (email newsletters, Tweets, blog posts, etc) and rewarding them with fresh content.

Remember: it costs you less to keep an existing customer happy than to acquire a new one.

WELCOME BACK

KEEP IN TOUCH

#81 Bounce Rates

The bounce rate, which you will see in your analytics package as a percentage, is the number of visitors who only visit one page of your website and leave immediately to another site. It should not be confused with 'exit rate', which is the percentage of visitors leaving from a given page compared to the total number of visitors to that page.

You can lower your bounce rates by:

Improving the page layout so it is clear and concise.

- - - - - - - - - -

Make sure your page is relevant and targeted to the audience.

- - - - - - - - - -

Ensure all your campaigns lead to the right page on your site.

- - - - - - - - - -

Split-test different options to find the best page for the audience.

Landing pages, particularly from paid ad campaigns (PPC), should have a low bounce rate. If not, it's likely they are under-performing.

Search is Changing

#82 Alternative Search Engines

For most of the last decade Google was unstoppable, and SEO became almost entirely focused on satisfying Google. However, the web is dynamic and inspires innovation. In recent months there have been some interesting new search engines entering the market

We now have:

- Visual search engines e.g. quintura.com, search-cube.com, kartoo.com.
- Social media search engines e.g. socialmention.com, whostalkin.com, samepoint.com.
- Video search engines e.g. youtube.com, dailymotion.com, blinkx.com, en.fooooo.com, truveo.com. In Dec 2008, Comscore claimed that 25% of all searches that Google processes come through their video site, YouTube.
- Knowledge engines e.g. wolframalpha.com.

If you want to reach an audience outside of the main search engines, it could be worth checking out the new engines most relevant to you.

#83 Search Goes Local

As well as opening up a global marketplace, the internet has also made it easier to find things on your own doorstep. The increasing use of mobile phones to find information has also increased the opportunity of being found by a highly relevant, locally based audience. For example, local searches may be at a national, e.g. 'car hire Spain', or more regional level, involving a specific location e.g. 'hotels in Bayswater'.

Don't miss out. Add your site to Google Maps, Google's Local Business Center, Windows Live Local and Yahoo! Local, and all relevant local directories and portals. These services use your postcode to place your business on the map, which will then appear in search results. Make sure you include all of your offices and branches to take full advantage.

#84 Mobile Search

Growth in the use of the mobile internet, and Google's continuing focus on mobile through its Android operating system and Nexus 1 Smartphone, means your website needs to be easy to find, and have fast load times, to satisfy the needs of mobile users.

There are many different types of mobile search from "Find my Nearest" services, mobile versions of the search engines, question and answer services, and directories.
We are also likely to see far more mobile advertising, including geo-locational advertising which targets users by their current location and recommends specific services that are in the vicinity.

Where To Go From Here

#85 Get In Step To The Google Dance

Being Number 1 in the SERPs (pronounced "surps") is the goal of every SEO. It is also the cause of multiple headaches, as there is often no obvious logic or reason why your site has suddenly plummeted from page 1 to page 30.

Should that happen to you – do not panic. The usual reason is a change in the algorithm or an update to the search engine's index, over which you have no control. The algorithms (the 'equation' which a search engine uses to define your ranking) are increasingly complex and changes or updates are commonly known as "The Google Dance".

If you have recently made major changes to the site, be patient. Don't immediately undo everything you have done. You made those changes for a reason, right? Wait and see whether your ranking returns. If, after a reasonable time, there is still no improvement, make incremental changes and observe the results.

ClickThrough
the search conversion experts

Ten Internet Marketing Commandments

Now your website is in place here are some sacrosanct laws of Internet Marketing that you should try to follow at all times:

1 Never assume you have made every change you can. Test, test, and test again. (See tips #78, #79 and #81)

2 Once you have made changes remember to monitor, evaluate, and if it isn't working, change it again.

3 Never do more than you can handle. The only way to eat an elephant is in small bites.

4 Think out of the box – be a guerrilla marketer and stand out from the crowd.

5 Search engine spiders will not buy from you. Your visitors will.

6 Be generous in sharing your expertise. A good reputation is worth more than a top 10 ranking any day.

7 Never, ever try to con the search engines.

8 What goes on online stays online – learn and practice netiquette (acceptable online behaviour).

9 Lurk before you leap e.g. take care to read forums before posting so you understand the type of people likely to reply.

10 Take internet marketing seriously. Your website needs time and resources spent to achieve the results you desire.

Click·Through
the search conversion experts

#96 Powerful Competitive Analysis

Don't ever take your eyes off your competitors. You can guarantee they are watching you. You can determine who your competitors are by looking who else is ranking for your major keywords, using business information tools such as Dun & Bradstreet, (DNB.com), the trade press for your sector, comparison sites, industry reports, and so on.

Analyse everything your competitors do - right and wrong. Press releases will indicate marketing activities, new clients, product launches, hires and fires, and more. Learn from their successes and failures. If your competitors have a great marketing idea, see how you can adapt it to serve your own customers.

Use tools such as popuri.us and browser plug-ins e.g. seoquake.com to quickly identify a competitor's ranking and backlinks. For in-depth reports, majesticseo.com allows advanced analysis of backlinks, authority, and anchor text usage. Tools such as keywordspy.com and spyfu.com can tell you the organic and paid keywords of importance to competitors.

Google Trends can help you to find competitors you were unaware of, as well as giving you data on your competitors' website traffic. Search for a known competitor using the 'website' option, and take note of all the sites listed under 'Also visited' and 'Also searched for'. You can drill down further by clicking on the links given.

Takeaways:

1. **Watch your competitors carefully.**
2. **Analyse and learn from their actions.**
3. **Adapt those actions to meet your own needs.**

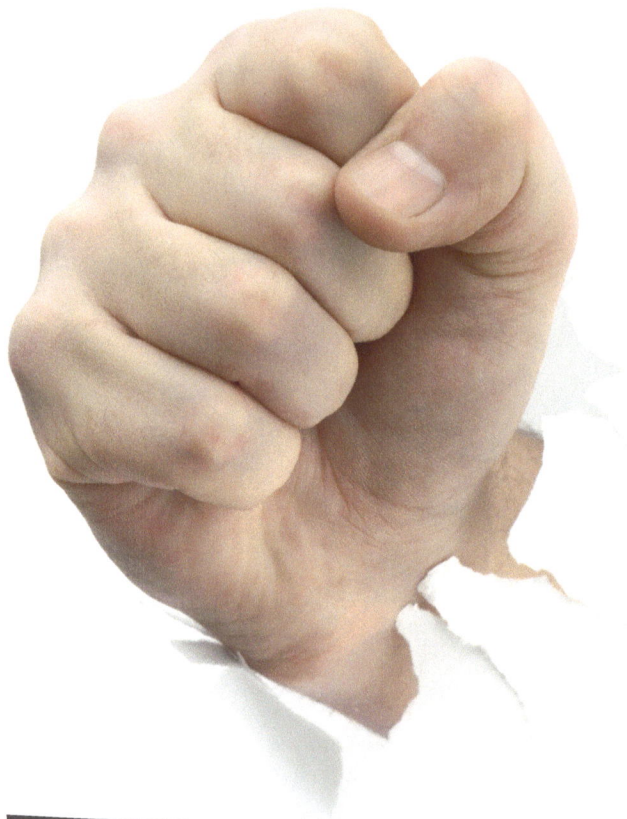

#97 Recording your Internet Marketing Activities

If you have followed even half of the tips in this book, you will have begun to conduct a thorough campaign to promote and market your website online. Many of your actions will be recorded within the tools that you have used, but others will have been spontaneous, or delivered manually.

Keep a record of all actions in a logical and structured manner, so that you can monitor exactly what results are coming from which actions. A simple spreadsheet is all you require to begin with. This will stop you from making duplicate posts to blogs, requesting a link multiple times, or submitting your site to the same directory twice.

ClickThrough
the search conversion experts

#98 Driving Web Traffic By Marketing Offline

As you can now see, there are multiple ways to drive traffic online, but there are also ways to bring traffic from offline sources too.

Here are just a few ideas which may also help raise awareness of your site and get you links through other websites you did not expect or request:

- Signwrite your vehicle and shop with your URL.
- Make sure your website address is on every piece of stationery and marketing collateral.
- Put your website address on your answerphone message.
- Write articles for magazines, which include a 'resource box', including your website address.
- Leave your business card everywhere you can.

#99 Choosing an Agency

For many companies, there simply is not the in-house resource or experience to deliver an effective, profitable online marketing campaign. For others, it is preferable to use experts, rather than train or employ staff to conduct website promotion.

Choosing an agency can be a minefield, with many new companies springing up daily claiming, for instance, to be able to get your website to the top of the search engines. Note: should any agency offer to do that for you, particularly within a short time-frame or for undefined keywords – head for the door and save your money.

Here's what to look for:

- A reputable, experienced agency will offer you references and examples of successful campaigns for you to check out.

- You get what you pay for. SEO is a time-consuming, lengthy process and requires a considerable number of hours and expertise to get it right. Cheap solutions may harm rather than benefit your company.

- Make sure any SEO agency explains in depth any recommendations or actions they have for your site. Transparency is key. Validate that information for yourself so you know that the agency will be carrying out the right activities for your company and website.

Create An SEO Centric Culture

To maximize your SEO investment, upskill your staff so that they can work more effectively with your agency. In order to develop a culture of SEO within your company, seek out agencies which will help to train your staff in SEO techniques. This way all but the most advanced aspects of SEO become second nature in-house when creating new marketing campaigns.

CONTINUING YOUR SEO
JOURNEY

Things change online all the time, even if the overall guiding principles remain true. To keep up with the latest techniques Google's Search Engine Optimization Guide is a must-read, as well as their Webmaster Guidelines which highlight specifics to Google search. Bing and Yahoo! also offer similar resources. In addition, many of the world's top SEO experts contribute to sites such as **seomoz.com**, **seobook.com** and **searchenginewatch.com**.

Finally, **Clickthrough-Marketing.com** has also produced a range of up to date guides to help you out, so check out our site.